FROM SEA to SHINING SEA

LOUISIANA

ELLEN MACAULAY

Consultants

MELISSA N. MATUSEVICH, PH.D.

Curriculum and Instruction Specialist
Blacksburg, Virginia

TERRENCE E. YOUNG, JR., M.ED., M.L.S.

Jefferson Parish Public School System
Louisiana

LINDA LINGEFELT

Library Media Specialist
Franklin Jr. High School
Franklin, Louisiana

CHILDREN'S PRESS®

A DIVISION OF SCHOLASTIC INC.

New York • Toronto • London • Auckland • Sydney • Mexico City
New Delhi • Hong Kong • Danbury, Connecticut

Louisiana is in the southern part of the United States. It is bordered by Mississippi, Arkansas, Texas, and the Gulf of Mexico.

The photograph on the front cover shows bald cypress trees in Atchafalaya Basin at sunset.

Project Editor: Meredith DeSousa
Art Director: Marie O'Neill
Photo Researcher: Marybeth Kavanagh
Design: Robin West, Ox and Company, Inc.
Page 6 map and recipe art: Susan Hunt Yule
All other maps: XNR Productions, Inc.

Library of Congress Cataloging-in-Publication Data

Macaulay, Ellen.
        Louisiana / Ellen Macaulay.
            p. cm. — (From sea to shining sea)
        Includes bibliographical references (p.) and index.
    ISBN 0-516-22399-2
        1. Louisiana—Juvenile literature. I. Title. II. Series.

F369.3 .M33 2003
976.3—dc21   2002015137

TABLE of CONTENTS

CHAPTER ONE

INTRODUCING THE PELICAN STATE

Louisiana's nickname comes from the brown pelican, which is also the state bird.

Louisiana is unlike anywhere else in the world. It has a unique blend of culture and heritage, making it one of the most interesting states in the nation. Louisiana's colorful history includes plantation ladies, voodoo queens, Creoles, and Cajuns. Its lively spirit comes from the snappy sounds of jazz and zydeco music. Louisiana is a place to have fun!

Louisiana is considered part of the Deep South. The weather is balmy, and the land is lush and green. Wildlife is abundant. Alligators enjoy lurking in its slow-moving waters. So did pirates, at one time.

Originally a territory of France, Louisiana was named in honor of French King Louis XIV. It became part of the United States in 1803, when President Thomas Jefferson bought the Louisiana Territory as part of a famous agreement called the Louisiana Purchase. The Louisiana Territory included much of what is now the central United States.

Today, Louisiana's claim to fame is music. The city of New Orleans is known as the birthplace of jazz—lively music that originated with African slaves and freedmen in the United States. Famous musicians with strange names such as Satchmo and Jelly Roll learned their craft in Louisiana, where the streets are always alive with music and dancing. You can hear jazz, blues, gospel, and rock and roll. There is something for everyone in Louisiana.

What else comes to mind when you think of Louisiana?

- French-speaking Cajun settlers who came long ago from Canada
- Delicious gumbo dishes
- Zydeco bands with accordions, guitars, drums, and old-fashioned washboards
- Cruising the marshlands for exotic birds or a sneaky alligator
- Cotton and sugarcane fields
- Vampires in an above-ground cemetery
- Relaxing with a tall lemonade on a lacy iron balcony overlooking the French Quarter
- Fancy costumes and festive parades during Mardi Gras
- Stately mansions in Plantation Country

Turn the page to discover more about this special state. You'll soon find that nothing compares to the sights, sounds, lore, and legend of Louisiana.

Shreveport

Monroe

Mississippi River

Baton Rouge

MARDI GRAS!

New Orleans

Lake Charles

Lafayette

©SHY 02

6

CHAPTER TWO

THE LAND OF LOUISIANA

Louisiana is easy to locate on a map because it is shaped like a boot. A Gulf Coast state, Louisiana's southern border is the Gulf of Mexico. Texas is to the west, Arkansas is to the north, and Mississippi is to the east. The Mississippi River forms the eastern border with Mississippi and the Sabine River forms part of the western border with Texas.

Louisiana was once entirely underwater as part of the Gulf of Mexico. Earth deposits, mainly from the Mississippi River, eventually built up the land to its present size. Land formations are still working their way up through the abundant wetlands in Louisiana, where 2,482 islands cover more than one million acres (404,700 hectares).

The sun sets over cypress swamps at Jean Lafitte National Historical Park and Preserve.

FIND OUT MORE

Louisiana ranks third nationwide in total number of islands. It ranks second in island acreage (a unit to measure land area). Which state(s) have even more islands?

There are three main land regions within Louisiana: the West Gulf Coastal Plain, the Mississippi Alluvial Plain, and the East Gulf Coastal Plain. Each region has distinct characteristics.

West Gulf Coastal Plain

Most of Louisiana lies in the West Gulf Coastal Plain, the area west of the Mississippi River and the surrounding Mississippi Alluvial Plain. The West Gulf Coastal Plain extends north to Arkansas, west to Texas, and south to the Gulf of Mexico.

The vast West Gulf Coastal Plain changes dramatically from place to place, and includes a variety of land formations. Barrier beaches lie along the Gulf of Mexico making up the southernmost region. Behind these sandy beaches are the swampy marshlands (wetlands) most commonly

The saltwater marshes of Sabine National Wildlife Refuge, located in southwestern Louisiana, provide a habitat for migratory waterfowl and other birds.

associated with a Deep South state. This southern region is brimming with shrimp, oysters, crabs, and crawfish, mostly harvested in the Atchafalaya Basin. Rice and oil are also plentiful.

Underground salt domes are often found beneath the marshlands. Salt domes are places where salt deposits have forced their way up through layers of rock, and rest just a few hundred feet below the earth's surface. The areas around these domes often contain natural gas, petroleum, and sulfur. Avery Island is one such dome. It is made of solid salt.

Heading north, the marshlands eventually disappear. Miles of prairies, or grasslands, take their place. The prairies gradually rise into rolling hills, then forests. The 600,000-acre (242,915-hectare) Kisatchie National Forest in central and northern Louisiana is blanketed with

FIND OUT MORE

Spanish moss is a plant that hangs on the branches and trunks of cypress trees found along the marshlands of the West Gulf Coastal Plain. It is not a true moss because it has no roots; it gets moisture and nutrients from the air. To what plant family does Spanish moss belong and to what other plant(s) is it related?

A group of bicyclists ride through Kisatchie National Park.

A group of bicyclists ride through Kisatchie National Park.

pine, oak, and maple trees. The northern part of the forest is called Sportsman's Paradise because it is a natural environment for fishing, hunting, and outdoor activities.

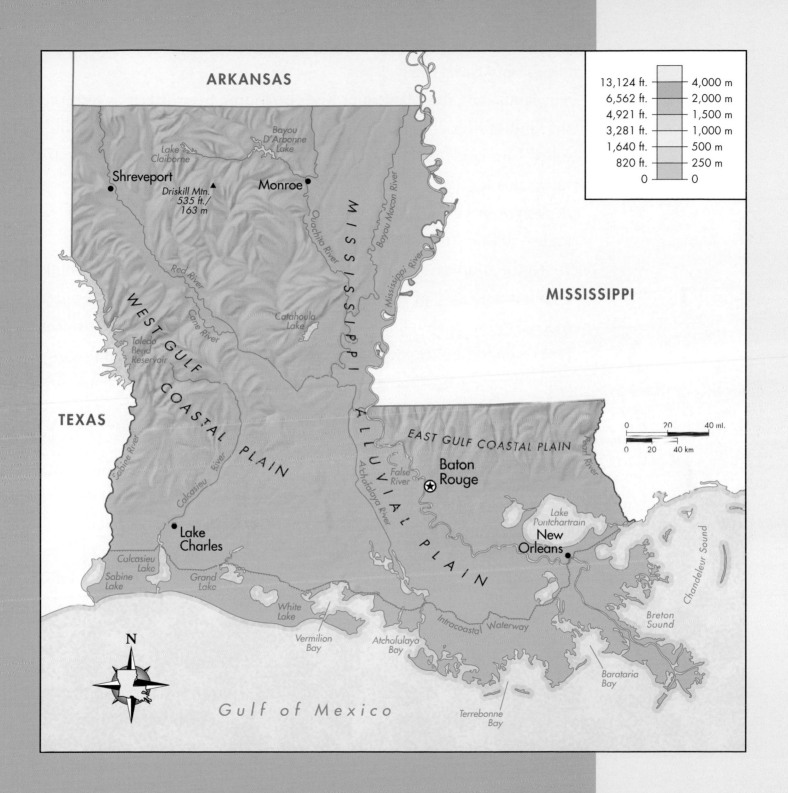

ARKANSAS

Bayou
D'Arbonne
Lake

Lake
Claiborne

Shreveport

Driskill Mtn.
535 ft./
163 m

Monroe

Ouachita River

Bayou Macon River

Mississippi River

MISSISSIPPI ALLUVIAL PLAIN

Red River

Cane River

Catahoula
Lake

WEST GULF COASTAL PLAIN

Toledo
Bend
Reservoir

TEXAS

Sabine River

MISSISSIPPI

EAST GULF COASTAL PLAIN

Pearl River

Baton
Rouge

False
River

Atchafalaya River

Lake
Pontchartrain

New
Orleans

Calcasieu River

Lake
Charles

Chandeleur Sound

Calcasieu
Lake

Sabine
Lake

Grand
Lake

White
Lake

Intracoastal Waterway

Breton
Sound

Barataria
Bay

Vermilion
Bay

Atchafalaya
Bay

Terrebonne
Bay

N

Gulf of Mexico

13,124 ft. — 4,000 m
6,562 ft. — 2,000 m
4,921 ft. — 1,500 m
3,281 ft. — 1,000 m
1,640 ft. — 500 m
820 ft. — 250 m
0 — 0

0   20   40 mi.

0   20   40 km

Mississippi Alluvial Plain

The land along the Mississippi River extending from Arkansas south to the Gulf of Mexico is the Mississippi Alluvial Plain. Low ridges of land, called frontlands, line the sides of the river. Beyond the frontlands are the backlands, large stretches of clay and silt soils. The traveling silt was deposited at the river's mouth centuries ago, forming the area now known as the Mississippi Delta.

To the southeast is the city of New Orleans. New Orleans was built on a natural curve of the Mississippi River. At an average of 8 feet (2.4 meters) below sea level, it is the lowest point in Louisiana. New Orleans is surrounded by freshwater and saltwater natural lakes, including the approximately 630-square mile (1,632-sq km) Lake Pontchartrain. Banana trees and blueberry patches are found in the outlying areas.

Cotton thrives in Louisiana's rich soil.

East Gulf Coastal Plain

East of the Mississippi River and north of Lake Pontchartrain is the East Gulf Coastal Plain. The marshlands to the west and north of Lake Pontchartrain gradually change to rolling hills. These hills extend north and continue up to the state of Mississippi.

The East Gulf Coastal Plain is a small area with rich farmland. Cotton and sugarcane thrive in this fertile soil, as did the indigo plant, whose leaves were used to dye clothes dark blue.

RIVERS AND LAKES

Water is everywhere in Louisiana. There are 6,084 square miles (9,813 sq km) of water surface. Louisiana alone contains almost half the coastal marshlands of the entire United States. There are numerous lakes, rivers, marshes, swamps, and bayous throughout Louisiana. Most of them have formed as overflow from the Mississippi River. Louisiana is often called the Bayou State because it has so many bayous.

The Mississippi River is a major waterway for many states. It is also the largest river in the United States. It flows 305 miles (492 kilometers) along Louisiana's eastern border, through Baton Rouge and New Orleans, finally merging with the Gulf of Mexico. The mighty Mississippi River floods frequently. For more than two hundred years, the riverbanks have been lined with structures called levees to hold back rising water. Although flooding is destructive, eventually some good comes out of it. Nutrient-rich

The Mississippi River forms a crescent shape at New Orleans.

soil is carried from the flood and deposited at the mouth of the river. This soil is the best in the world for growing crops.

The Red River and the Atchafalaya River are other major rivers in Louisiana. The Red River flows through the center of Louisiana in the West Gulf Coastal Plain. It flows through northern forests of cypress, oak, and gum trees.

The Red River feeds into the Atchafalaya River to the south. The Atchafalaya River provides a natural border between the Mississippi Alluvial Plain to the east and the swampy West Gulf Coastal Region to the south. Also in the West Gulf Coastal Region, the Calcasieu River runs through the town of Lake Charles to Calcasieu Lake. In the westernmost part of Louisiana, the Sabine River empties into Sabine Lake, and then into the Gulf of Mexico.

In the Mississippi Alluvial Plain, the Pearl River flows down from the state of Mississippi, filling many natural lakes. In the East Gulf Coastal Plain, the False River branches off from the Mississippi River above Baton Rouge.

CLIMATE

As a southern state, Louisiana has a warm, humid subtropical climate year-round, with mild winters and hot summers. The average winter temperatures are 55° Fahrenheit (13° Celsius) in the southern part of the state and 49° F (9° C) in the north. The average summer temperature is 82° F (28° C) throughout the state. The temperature once reached a record high of 114° F (46° C) at Plain Dealing in 1936. Louisiana's climate is extremely humid (moist), which makes it feel even hotter.

Louisiana gets about 57 inches (2 centimeters) of rain per year. The rain keeps the state lush and green. Louisiana also gets many tropical storms, including destructive hurricanes. Rotating winds of more than 74 miles per hour (119 kilometers per hour) accompany fierce rain and severe thunderstorms. As one of the flattest states, Louisiana is at an increased risk for hurricanes. (Hurricanes have the chance to pick up speed in flat areas.) About 30 hurricanes and 55 tropical storms have descended upon Louisiana in the past one hundred years. Most have hit coastal areas along the Gulf of Mexico.

In October 2002, Hurricane Lili brought heavy wind and rain to some parts of Louisiana.

FIND OUT MORE

The spoonbill is a most unusual bird. It looks like a combination of a pink flamingo and a pelican. How do its strange features, such as its shovel-like beak, help this bird survive in Louisiana?

Louisiana is officially called the Pelican State after its state bird, the native brown pelican. Brown pelicans flock to this water wonderland, along with other magnificent birds such as snowy egrets, eagles, herons and ducks. The vast Gulf Coastline is home to many beautiful shorebirds. The marshlands of Louisiana provide a resting place for millions of migratory birds. Migratory birds range from the large Canadian goose to the very small hummingbird.

The natural splendors of Louisiana provide a treat for all your senses. Sniff the magnolia blossoms, feel the squish of swampland beneath your feet, and listen to the howl of the Catahoula Hound. You're in Louisiana!

CHAPTER THREE
LOUISIANA THROUGH HISTORY

The first people came to Louisiana more than 12,000 years ago. Called hunters and gatherers, they migrated from the north and survived by hunting animals and gathering plants. Scientists have studied spears and tools that these prehistoric people left behind. Ferocious saber-toothed tigers were just one of many dangers they faced every day.

Poverty Point village, located alongside the Mississippi River in northeast Louisiana, is the oldest known civilization in Louisiana, dating back at least 3,000 years. This village provides evidence of a group of people called Mound Builders. They were called Mound Builders because they built towering mounds—some as tall as modern-day office buildings—made from dirt and mud. Some mounds can still be seen today throughout Louisiana, in New Orleans, Marksville, and Poverty Point near Epps.

Mardi Gras has a long history in Louisiana.

FIND OUT MORE

Archaeologists—scientists who study early cultures—are not certain what purpose the mounds served. They have uncovered bones, tools, and pottery in and around the mounds. Scientists can study these items to learn more about these early people and their culture. What do you think the mounds may have been used for?

Another early settlement in Louisiana dates back more than 2,000 years. A group of people whom French explorers called Tunica built a settlement at Marksville. The French admired the Tunica's business skills as well as their peaceful nature. Today, Tunica descendants still live on government-protected tribal lands in Marksville. The Tunica-Biloxi Indian Museum holds a large collection of Native American and European artifacts.

As far back as A.D. 600, the Choctaw, Chickasaw, and other Native Americans lived in the swampy Barataria region in southern Louisiana. Shell tools and ceremonial burial mounds that have been found among the bayous help scientists piece together the puzzle of their existence.

Early Native Americans created settlements along the Mississippi River.

Other groups also settled in Louisiana. The Caddo lived in the northwest, in the Natchitoches region. The Houma lived in the northern Barataria region. The Bayou Goula and Chitimacha lived in the south, west of the Mississippi River. The Acolapissa and Attakapa lived in the far southwest areas of Louisiana.

These Native American groups were farmers who grew corn and beans. Other food sources included deer, bears, fish, and clams. Artifacts show that these groups formed complex societies relating to art, religion, government, gardening, and trading. Most people lived in villages in sturdy houses of wood, leaves, moss, and mud.

La Salle dreamed of creating a French empire in the New World.

EUROPEAN EXPLORATION

The Native American way of life changed forever with the arrival of European explorers. Spanish explorer Alonso Alvarez de Pineda led an expedition along the Gulf of Mexico and came upon the mouth of the Mississippi River in 1519. In 1541, another Spanish explorer named Hernando De Soto came in search of gold. He never found it. De Soto died the next year and was buried in the Mississippi River.

In 1682, French fur trader René-Robert Cavelier, Sieur de La Salle canoed down to the mouth of the Mississippi River. He stuck a cross in the mud and claimed the entire Mississippi River Valley for the king of France, Louis XIV—something the Spanish explorers never thought of doing. This began the struggle between France and Spain for possession of Louisiana and the surrounding territory. To both the French and Spanish, land ownership represented power.

In 1699, Louisiana became a French royal colony, which meant that it was controlled by the king of France. Fifteen years later, in 1714, Louis Juchereau de St. Denis of France established Louisiana's first European settlement on the Red River. It was called Natchitoches, named for the Natchitoches Indian tribe. In 1718, New Orleans (called *Nouvelle Orléans* in French) was built on a gentle curve of the Mississippi River. It was an immediately popular destination with the French and other Europeans. Its location near the Gulf of Mexico made it a natural shipping port and easy to reach. A French-Canadian explorer, Jean Baptiste le Moyne, Sieur de Bienville, saw its potential and developed New Orleans as a fur-trading community.

This illustration shows a view of New Orleans in 1718.

In 1719, French soldiers founded Baton Rouge. (*Baton Rouge* is French for "red stick," after the tale of a pole stained with animal blood that served as the dividing line between the Houmas and Bayou Goula Indians). By 1720, the French began logging trees through-out Louisiana to make cabins and boats.

Settlers from Europe and the East Coast arrived and settled in different areas. Early settlements had a lot to offer. There was plenty of food and water, wide-open spaces for shelter, and animal furs to trade.

Some Native American groups interacted with the new settlers. The Houmas, for example, taught settlers how to use the resources around them. They built boats, called pirogues, from cypress trees. They used cane reeds and feathers to make clothing and baskets. Eventually, most settlers and Native Americans adapted to each other's presence. Some even married and had children together.

Still, many people died in those early days. Native Americans died from strange diseases transmitted by the settlers. In turn, settlers didn't have the experience needed to survive tough conditions, including bad weather and dangerous wild animals.

NEW WORLD CULTURES

As the settlements grew, agriculture (farming) became the main focus. To provide cheap labor for Louisiana farms, massive numbers of

Many Louisiana farms depended on slave labor.

Africans and Caribbeans were brought to Louisiana by force as part of the French slave trade. Most slaves came from Senegambia, between Africa's Senegal and Gambia rivers, a land rich with crops, livestock, and industry.

Many slave owners were cruel and unfeeling. Slaves were treated like property and could be bought or sold. Often, slave families were split apart. Some courageous slaves ran away, but those who were caught were brutally beaten. In 1720, a settlement for runaway African slaves was established at

EXTRA! EXTRA!

In the late-1700s, a former slave named Marie Therese Coincoin turned a small plot of land in northwest Louisiana into the thriving Yucca Plantation (later called the Melrose Plantation). Marie Therese, as well as her children and grandchildren, became wealthy as a result of the plantation's success. More than one hundred years later, in the 1880s, John and Cammie Henry bought the estate and turned it into a creative community where artists and writers could work and pursue their interests. Famous writers William Faulkner and John Steinbeck were among the many guests at Melrose's "Big House."

Bayou Lacombe. It was the first of the "free" establishments, where protected slaves were allowed to form their own communities.

Over the years, a new ethnic group called the Creoles developed in Louisiana. Creoles were native-born descendants of Europeans, particularly French and Spanish settlers. Creoles took pride in being born in the colony, unlike many European settlers. They made food, clothing, and music that was uniquely theirs.

Soon, another new culture emerged called the Cajuns. In 1755, French-speaking Acadians were forced to leave Acadia (present-day Nova Scotia in Canada) for refusing to give up their Catholic religion as required by British rule. Homeless Acadians wandered for ten years down the East Coast. Families were separated and more than half of the exiled Acadians died during their journey. Between 1764 and 1788, they arrived in New Orleans.

The Louisiana government provided the new arrivals with food, tools, and land. The Acadians (shortened to *Cajuns*) settled along the isolated swamplands of southern Louisiana, where towns such as Vermilionville were formed. To feed their families, they farmed rice, hot peppers, and

Acadians were herded onto ships and forced out of eastern Canada in 1755.

okra. Like the Creoles, they used these foods to develop a unique style of cooking. The Cajuns and Creoles are two of few cultures truly born in the United States.

In 1762, the Spanish gained control of Louisiana and the surrounding territory. French rebels attempted a takeover in 1768, but Spanish forces under the leadership of General Alexander "Bloody" O'Reilly put a stop to the rebellion. (O'Reilly earned his nickname because he harshly punished the captured leaders of the revolt.) The Spanish held on to Louisiana for more than thirty years. During this time, Spanish law, language, and architecture replaced those of the French.

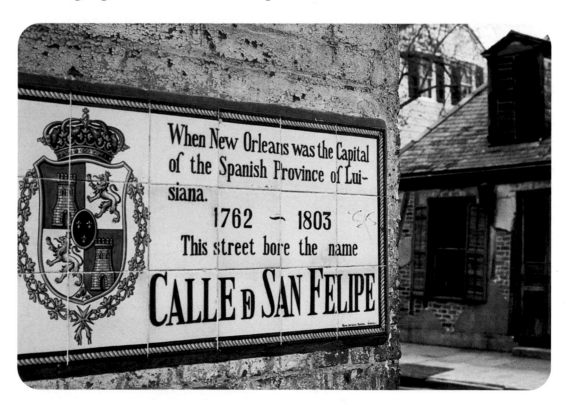

Reminders of Spanish rule can still be seen in some parts of Louisiana.

Spanish rulers eventually tired of governing a far-off territory. They were fearful of another revolution by restless and angry colonists. In 1800, Spain returned the territory to the French. Just three years later, in 1803, France sold the Louisiana Territory to the United States for $15 million. Called the Louisiana Purchase, the new land—which included all the land west of the Mississippi River to the Rocky Mountains—doubled the size of the United States. It included most of Louisiana as well as what would become several other states, as far north as Montana.

FIND OUT MORE

Draw a map of the land area included in the Louisiana Purchase. What other present-day states did it include?

William Claiborne was appointed governor of the Louisiana Territory by President Thomas Jefferson.

FROM TERRITORY TO STATEHOOD

William Charles Cole Claiborne was the first governor of the new United States territory. Claiborne faced many challenges during his term as governor. The Creoles didn't like him because he couldn't speak French. At the same time, President Thomas Jefferson insisted that Louisiana be more "Americanized" and not speak so much French. In addition, Claiborne also worried about disputes with Spain over the Gulf of Mexico border. Claiborne's most memorable act as governor was when he declared that his favorite animal, the pelican, be placed on all official correspondence. In 1902, this image was made the state seal.

General Andrew Jackson led the charge at the Battle of New Orleans.

During this time, more people streamed into the new territory. New Orleans, with its fine dining, colorful people, and cultural events, became a major tourist attraction. Europeans called it the European Queen of the Mississippi.

In 1810, the Louisiana Territory gained strength and land when the "Florida Parishes" (areas in present-day eastern Louisiana and Florida) successfully rose up against Spain. Louisiana's population grew to 76,556, enough to meet the United States Congress' standards for statehood. On April 30, 1812, Louisiana became the eighteenth state.

Soon after, Louisiana became involved in the War of 1812 (1812–1815), between the United States and Great Britain. In late 1814, thousands of British soldiers tried to capture New Orleans. To protect the city, Major General Andrew Jackson assembled Louisiana troops made up of trained soldiers, Native Americans, slaves, free African-Americans, and even pirates. On January 8, 1815, they fought at Chalmette to win the Battle of New Orleans, only to discover that the War of 1812 was already over.

The year of 1812 brought another notable event: the first steamboat to travel down the Mississippi River. It was called the *New Orleans,* and was the first of many steamboats. Steamboat travel was valuable because it offered a faster and easier method of transportation. This meant more opportunities for selling and buying cotton, Louisiana's most important crop.

By the mid 1800s, cotton and sugar plantations were flourishing in Louisiana. Plantations were large farms that grew one main crop, usually cotton or sugar. With free slave labor, some plantation owners became wealthy, but wealth offered little protection against disease. In 1853, the yellow fever plague hit Louisiana hard. The disease was spread far and wide by swamp mosquitoes, and people died faster

WHO'S WHO IN LOUISIANA?

Jean Lafitte (1780–1826) was a pirate who helped defeat the British in the Battle of New Orleans. Leader of a gang of pirates, his illegal operation was located near New Orleans on the Baratarian Coast. He gathered a large crew of fellow pirates known as Baratarians to help him fight for the Americans. After the war, Lafitte was considered a hero and pardoned for any former crimes. The town of Lafitte is named after him.

Many religious leaders cared for the poor and sick during the yellow fever outbreak.

than graves could be dug. More than 11,000 people died in New Orleans alone.

THE CIVIL WAR

By the mid-1800s, Louisiana was one of many southern states that made money by farming. In contrast, Northerners found other ways to make money. Manufacturing (the making of products) was a large part of the economy there. The manufacturing industry provided jobs—and wages—for a large number of workers. Many Northerners did not believe in slave labor; in fact, slavery was illegal in many northern states.

The debate over slavery caused much tension between the North and South. The issue became even more important in 1860, when Abraham Lincoln was elected president of the United States. President Lincoln was against the spread of slavery. Many Southerners felt threatened by this, believing that Lincoln would try to put an end to slavery. They felt they had the right to decide whether slavery should be permitted within their own state. In general, many Southerners felt strongly about state's rights, or the idea that each state should be able to make its own laws.

By 1861, North and South were completely divided. Lincoln wanted to preserve the United States because he knew that a united country would be a far greater power than two separate countries. The southern states refused to listen to Lincoln's pleas. Instead, they began to secede, or leave, the United States. Louisiana supported slave ownership, and in January 1861 Louisiana seceded from the Union. Between

December 1860 and June 1861, ten other southern states also seceded. Together they formed their own nation called the Confederate States of America.

A short time later, the Civil War (1861–1865) broke out between the North and South. About 65,000 soldiers from Louisiana fought for the Confederacy against the Union (Northern) forces. In 1862, New Orleans and Baton Rouge were captured by Union forces. In 1863, Louisiana set a record for the longest siege in American military history when Confederates prevented Union troops from entering Port Hudson for forty-eight days. The Confederates were finally forced to give up the fight for Port Hudson, marking the end of Confederate control of the Mississippi River. However, the Confederates gained a victory when they crushed a Union advance on Shreveport.

Over time, military power and resources grew extremely scarce. Homes, schools, and churches were pressed into service as military quarters for soldiers and hospitals for the injured. Huge masonry forts such as Fort Pike were used to guard naval approaches to New Orleans because the city was vulnerable to attack from all sides.

In March 1863, the Union Navy Fleet attacked Confederate batteries at Port Hudson in Louisiana.

In 1865, the Confederate Army surrendered. The war was over. Louisiana, along with other southern states, set about rejoining the United States. They changed their state laws to go along with those required by the United States government. Slavery was now illegal, and all southern slaves were freed. Louisiana was readmitted to the Union in 1868. Union troops stayed in the area until 1877 to enforce the new laws.

RECONSTRUCTION

Much of the South suffered damage as a result of the war. Not only were its cities and towns in ruins, but its economy also suffered as slaves were freed and the plantation system broke down. The years after the Civil War are often referred to as Reconstruction, a time when the South was rebuilt.

After the slaves were freed, Southern landowners were left with lots of land, but little money to pay for laborers. They often took advantage of the newly freed slaves and poor European Americans through sharecropping. Landowners rented their land to these farmers in return for a share of the crops. These renters were called tenant farmers or, more commonly, sharecroppers. The landlord sold the crops and shared the profit

A sharecropper settles his claims at the general store.

with farmers, but only after subtracting the cost of supplies, food, and housing. Most sharecroppers ended up with barely enough to live on.

African-Americans made some progress in other areas. At the Louisiana Constitutional Convention of 1868, half the delegates were African-American. Also, the thirteenth amendment was created to officially abolish slavery. Louisiana's first African-American governor, P. B. S. Pinchback, served from 1872 to 1873.

EXTRA! EXTRA!

More than sixty years before the Colfax and Caldonia Massacres, the largest slave uprising in history took place in southwestern Louisiana. Called the Slave Insurrection of 1811, five hundred slaves fought to free themselves and others, but local military forces defeated them.

On April 13, 1873, progress came to a halt. A riot erupted in Colfax between a group called the White League and Louisiana's African-American militia. More than sixty African-Americans were killed, while only three members of the White League died. This incident is referred to as the Colfax Massacre. A similar riot called the Caldonia Massacre broke out just five years later.

Shreveport was a busy shipping center in the mid-1800s.

DISCOVERIES

In the late 1800s, Louisiana experienced growth in industry and population. Cotton and sugar remained important crops. Mechanical devices such as the cotton gin replaced the hand labor of slaves. The cotton gin was a machine that separated the seeds from the cotton. This invention allowed for the mass production of cotton, making it an extremely profitable crop. The steamboat industry was also going strong. Washington became the largest steamboat port between New Orleans and St. Louis, Missouri.

In 1901, another Louisiana treasure hunt was underway. That year, oil was discovered outside of Jennings. Oil was also found in many other places in Louisiana, as was another valuable resource—natural gas. The state's first natural gas pipeline brought gas from the Caddo Field to Shreveport.

The early 1900s brought another important development—jazz music. It is thought that this style of music started long before the Civil War in New Orleans' Congo Square, an open-air market where slaves gathered on Sundays for song and dance. It was an African custom to play slow, mournful music on the way to funerals, and lively, brassy music afterwards. The purpose of the lively "jazzy" music was to celebrate the deceased person's welcome into heaven. Over time, African-Americans passed on their musical traditions, and soon the sweet sound of jazz was everywhere. Known as the Louisiana sound, jazz music caught on with fans around the world and remains immensely popular today.

In 1914, World War I (1914–1918) broke out in Europe. The United States did not immediately join the war. However, many American states produced war products to help France and England in the fight against Germany and Austria-Hungary. In 1917, after United States submarines were sunk by German forces, the United States entered into World War I.

Ten years later, a period of difficult financial times overwhelmed the United States. During what became known as the Great Depression (1929–1939), the value of money dropped dramatically. As a result, many people could no longer afford to buy the things they needed, including necessities such as food. Without anyone to buy their products, many companies were forced to close down. People all over the United States lost their jobs, and farm prices fell in Louisiana.

The Great Depression gradually came to an end as World War II (1939–1945) began. The United States entered the war in December 1941, when, in a sneak attack, Japanese aircraft bombed a United States naval base at Pearl Harbor in Hawaii. More than

WHAT'S IN A NAME?

Some Louisiana names have interesting origins.

Name	Comes From or Means
Atchafalaya	Native American word meaning "long river"
Barataria	French word for "dishonesty at sea;" refers to pirates who lived there
Baton Rouge	French words for "red stick," which divided the lands of two Native American groups
Cajun	Shortened version of Acadian, the name for French-Canadians from Acadia (Nova Scotia)
Creole	Variation of Spanish word criollo, for "white child born in the colonies"
Louisiana	Name given to the territory by René-Robert Cavelier, Sieur de La Salle for King Louis XIV of France
Mardi Gras	French for "Fat Tuesday"
Tunica	French for Marksville Native Americans, meaning "the people"

250,000 Louisiana soldiers served overseas in World War II. Back home, Louisiana's oil industries helped fill the wartime need for more metal and fuel. Higgins Industries in New Orleans built thousands of landing boats that helped to win the war. Suddenly, there were more jobs and more money for the Louisiana people.

WAR ON THE HOME FRONT: CIVIL RIGHTS

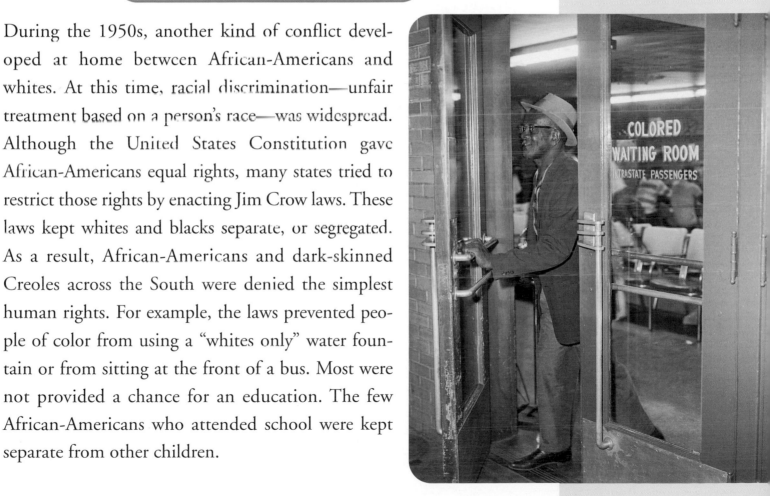

The term "colored" was used to label African-American facilities.

During the 1950s, another kind of conflict developed at home between African-Americans and whites. At this time, racial discrimination—unfair treatment based on a person's race—was widespread. Although the United States Constitution gave African-Americans equal rights, many states tried to restrict those rights by enacting Jim Crow laws. These laws kept whites and blacks separate, or segregated. As a result, African-Americans and dark-skinned Creoles across the South were denied the simplest human rights. For example, the laws prevented people of color from using a "whites only" water fountain or from sitting at the front of a bus. Most were not provided a chance for an education. The few African-Americans who attended school were kept separate from other children.

On June 7, 1892, an African-American named Homer Plessy was arrested for refusing to move from a "whites only" railcar. He wanted to challenge the Louisiana Separate Car Law, a Jim Crow law that said African-Americans could not ride in the same section as whites. Plessy's case went all the way to the United States Supreme Court. However, the Court ruled against Plessy and stated that "separate but equal" schools and public facilities were legal. This meant that even though slavery was outlawed, African-Americans' basic freedoms could still be restricted.

By the early 1960s, some Americans began speaking out against this unfair treatment of African-Americans. As part of the Civil Rights movement, many nonviolent protests took place in Louisiana. In 1960, hundreds of Southern University students in Baton Rouge gathered together and held up signs to protest unequal treatment at a Kress Department Store, where an African-American was arrested for sitting at a "whites only" lunch counter. After several court trials, the United States Supreme Court decided this man was innocent. This was the first case in which the Supreme Court sided with an African-American.

By 1974, most Jim Crow laws were legally overturned. A new state constitution was approved, one that fairly reflected the needs of all the people. This constitution still stands today.

African-American students protested segregation laws in Baton Rouge.

WE RESOLVE TO STAND UP IN THE FACE OF INTIMIDATION

Racial conflicts, poverty, pollution, and crime still play a role in modern life. However, history has proven that Louisiana always bounces back from its problems, and it will continue to do so.

Today, Louisiana proudly celebrates its diversity. Early German, Irish, and Spanish settlers all had an impact on Louisiana, as did the Creoles and Cajuns with their zesty way of life. The French language is still an important part of local culture. Although African-Americans did not come by choice, as many European immigrants did, they maintained their traditions and contributed greatly to society. Filipino, Chinese, and Hispanic families, along with others, add to the rich "melting pot" that is modern Louisiana.

Like these Cajuns, many Louisianans carry on the traditions of their culture.

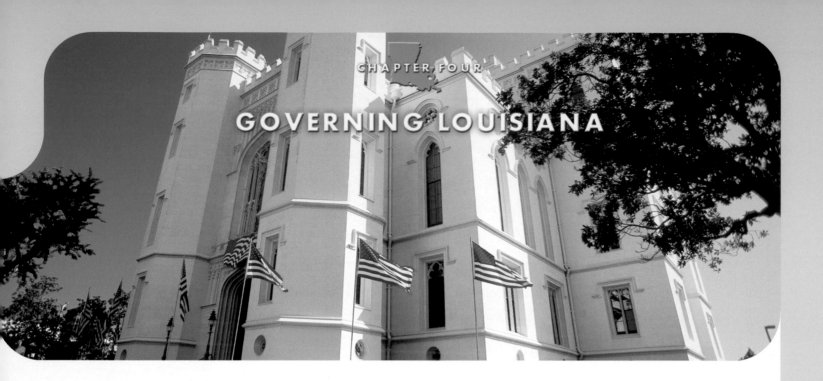

CHAPTER FOUR

GOVERNING LOUISIANA

The distinctive Old State Capitol building stands high atop the city of Baton Rouge.

The state constitution is important when it comes to governing Louisiana. A constitution provides written guidelines and laws for governing a group of people. Louisiana has had eleven constitutions since entering the Union—more than any other state. The constitution changed as people's view of government changed. The 1921 constitution set a record as the longest constitution in the United States. The present constitution was adopted in 1974. Once a constitution is in place, parts of it may still be changed, or amended, by a vote of the people.

Louisiana's constitution determines that there are three branches, or parts, to the state government. They are the executive branch, the legislative branch, and the judicial branch. The legislative branch makes laws, the executive branch enforces laws, and the judicial branch interprets, or explains, the laws. Each of these branches work together to make sure the state runs smoothly.

EXECUTIVE BRANCH

The executive branch is responsible for enforcing the laws of the state. It consists of the governor, lieutenant governor, secretary of state, attorney general, treasurer, and commissioners of agriculture and insurance. These officials are elected by the people of Louisiana, and each serves a four-year term.

The governor is head of the executive branch. The governor and other executive branch officials have numerous responsibilities, many of which involve raising money for the state. Governmental officials must decide on funding for schools, public safety, highways, natural disasters, insurance, environment, farming, and business dealings.

The governor is also involved in passing new laws. He or she has the power of veto, which means the governor may refuse to approve a proposed law even though lawmakers voted in favor of it. Louisiana State governors may only serve two terms, or eight years, in a row, but may serve additional terms later if re-elected.

The lieutenant governor acts as the governor's assistant as well as the head of the Department of Culture, Recreation, and Tourism. In

LOUISIANA GOVERNORS

Name	Term	Name	Term
W. C. C. Claiborne	1812–1816	Francis T. Nicholls	1888–1892
Jacques Villere	1816–1820	Murphy J. Foster	1892–1900
Thomas B. Robertson	1820–1824	William W. Heard	1900–1904
Henry S. Thibodaux	1824	Newton C. Blanchard	1904–1908
Henry Johnson	1824–1828	Jared Y. Sanders	1908–1912
Pierre Derbigny	1828–1829	Luther E. Hall	1912–1916
Armand Beauvais	1829–1830	Ruffin G. Pleasant	1916–1920
Jacques Dupré	1830–1831	John M. Parker	1920–1924
André B. Roman	1831–1835	Henry L. Fuqua	1924–1926
Edward D. White	1835–1839	Oramel H. Simpson	1926–1928
André B. Roman	1839–1843	Huey P. Long	1928–1932
Alexandre Mouton	1843–1846	Alvin O. King	1932
Isaac Johnson	1846–1850	Oscar K. Allen	1932–1936
Joseph Walker	1850–1853	James A. Noe	1936
Paul O. Hebert	1853–1856	Richard W. Leche	1936–1939
Robert C. Wickliffe	1856–1860	Earl K. Long	1939–1940
Thomas O. Moore	1860–1862	Sam H. Jones	1940–1944
Federal Military Rule	1862–1864	Jimmie H. Davis	1944–1948
Henry W. Allen	1864–1865	Earl K. Long	1948–1952
Michael Hahn	1864–1865	Robert F. Kennon	1952–1956
James M. Wells	1865–1867	Earl K. Long	1956–1960
Benjamin Flanders	1867–1868	Jimmie H. Davis	1960–1964
Joshua Baker	1868	John J. McKeithen	1964–1972
Henry C. Warmoth	1868–1872	Edwin W. Edwards	1972–1980
John McEnery	1872	David C. Treen	1980–1984
P. B. S. Pinchback	1872–1873	Edwin W. Edwards	1984–1988
William P. Kellogg	1873–1877	Buddy Roemer	1988–1992
Francis T. Nicholls	1877–1880	Edwin W. Edwards	1992–1996
Louis A. Wiltz	1880–1881	Murphy J. (Mike) Foster, Jr.	1996–2004
Samuel D. McEnery	1881–1888		

addition, the lieutenant governor takes over for the governor if he or she cannot serve for any reason.

LEGISLATIVE BRANCH

The legislative branch has an important job. It is Louisiana's lawmaking group. Every state needs rules to help it run as smoothly as possible. Members of the legislative branch, called legislators, create new laws about crime, the environment, taxes, traffic/vehicles, commendations (such as honoring a local hero), and other issues that affect Louisiana. Although the governor may veto a law, or refuse to approve it, the legislative branch can still pass it if two-thirds of the members vote to do so.

The legislative branch is made up of two parts: the senate and the house of representatives. There are 39 senate members, each representing one senatorial district. There are 105 members of the house of representatives, each representing one district. Elected by Louisiana voters, each member of the legislative branch serves a four-year term.

Inside the capitol, the senate chamber serves as a meeting place for Louisiana state senators.

Legislators also propose changes, called amendments, to the state constitution. Amendments must be approved by at least two-thirds of both legislative houses (senators and representatives). Amendments are then presented for a statewide election.

JUDICIAL BRANCH

The judicial branch is responsible for interpreting, or explaining, laws. This is done through the court system. The judicial branch includes forty district courts, five courts of appeal, and the state supreme court.

Many cases begin in district court. District courts hear both civil and criminal cases. Civil cases involve private disputes over property, documents, and labor, among other things. Criminal cases involve the breaking of a law, such as murder or theft.

If a person is not satisfied with the district court's decision in his or her case, he or she may ask for an appeal from a higher court. An appeal is an attempt to change a decision or ruling that was made in a lower court. If the higher court determines that a mistake was made during the trial, then the decision may be reviewed. The court of appeals handles many of these requests.

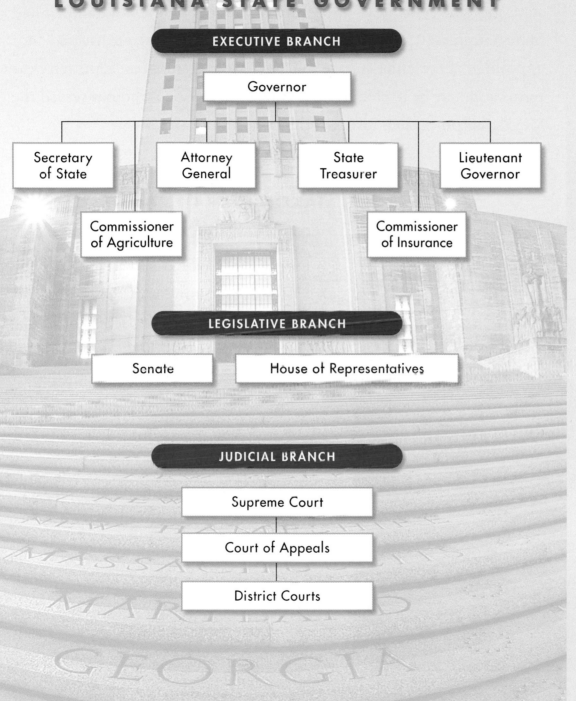

LOUISIANA STATE GOVERNMENT

EXECUTIVE BRANCH

Governor

Secretary of State

Attorney General

State Treasurer

Lieutenant Governor

Commissioner of Agriculture

Commissioner of Insurance

LEGISLATIVE BRANCH

Senate

House of Representatives

JUDICIAL BRANCH

Supreme Court

Court of Appeals

District Courts

The highest court is the state supreme court in New Orleans. The state supreme court hears appeals from lower courts. Unlike the United States Supreme Court, all Louisiana justices (judges) are elected, not appointed. One chief justice and six associate justices serve ten-year terms and may be re-elected many times. The justice who has served the longest becomes chief justice if the opportunity arises.

More than 227,000 people call Baton Rouge home.

TAKE A TOUR OF BATON ROUGE, THE STATE CAPITAL

Louisiana has had five capitals. New Orleans, Donaldsonville, Opelousas, and Shreveport were all capitals before Baton Rouge, which was chosen for its central location in 1846. The capital was moved to New Orleans during the Civil War, but in 1882 Baton Rouge was once again selected as the permanent capital of Louisiana.

The Old State Capitol, completed in 1849, looks like a castle. Civil War prisoners were held there until the building was damaged by fire in 1862. The Old State Capitol was reopened to the public in 1994 after much renovation of its fancy marble, wood, and tile. It is one of America's architectural treasures. The Old State Capitol now houses an interactive museum about the history of Louisiana's government.

The present capitol was completed in 1932. The tallest of the nation's capitols, it is thirty-four stories high. The view of the Mississippi River from the twenty-seventh floor observation deck is spectacular.

The names of each state are engraved on 48 steps outside the capitol entrance. (The names of Hawaii and Alaska were added later.) The house of representatives and the senate meet inside the capitol. Visitors can tour their chambers and learn about the architecture and history of the capitol building.

With its shady trees, green fields, and sleepy bayous, Baton Rouge is where Louisiana's plantation period comes alive. In fact, Baton Rouge and the surrounding area is sometimes called Plantation Country. In and around Baton Rouge you'll find beautifully restored mansions where wealthy plantation owners once ruled the land. Take in the grand mansions, then visit the slave cabins to see how the other half lived. One-room schools for plantation children

The names of each state are carved into the capitol steps in the order of their admittance into the Union.

and houses for the overseer (the person in charge of supervising the slaves) are also open to the public.

As well as being the center of government, Baton Rouge is a college town bustling with cultural events, activities, and enthusiastic young people. Louisiana State University and Southern University are both located there. Louisiana State houses the Rural Life Museum, which shows how plantations operated. Going back even farther in time, there are several Native American villages complete with ancient mud mounds in the greater Baton Rouge area.

Other interesting museums include the Louisiana Arts and Science Center and the Enchanted Mansion. The Arts and Science Center has a workshop and hands-on play area. The Enchanted Mansion is a doll museum that features a world-class doll collection and special activities for children.

Ice hockey fans have something to cheer about in Baton Rouge. The Baton Rouge Kingfish, named in honor of former Louisiana governor Huey "Kingfish" Long, play professional ice hockey at the Riverside Centroplex Arena. Each home game offers exciting hockey, plus laser light shows, music, and contests.

There's more fun to be had at Louisiana's largest water park. Blue Bayou Water Park has twelve waterslides, a wave pool, and its own river. It's a great way to cool off in sticky summer weather.

WHO'S WHO IN LOUISIANA?

Huey "Kingfish" Long (1893–1935) served as governor of Louisiana from 1928 to 1932, and a United States senator from 1932 to 1935. He was a colorful and popular leader. One of his programs provided free textbooks for schoolchildren. Long also helped to develop the state. However, as a result of some dishonest political activities, Long made many enemies. He was planning to run for president when, in 1935, he was assassinated at the capitol building. Long was born in Winnfield.

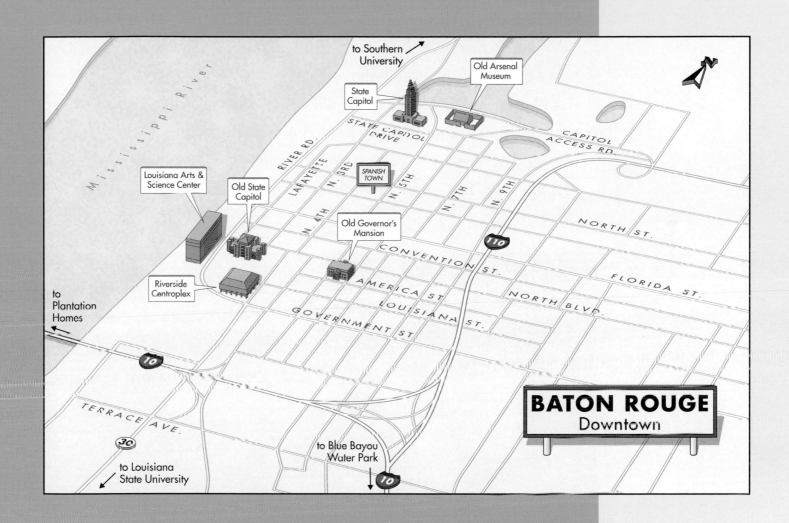

to Southern
University

Old Arsenal
Museum

State
Capitol

Mississippi River

STATE CAPITOL DRIVE

Louisiana Arts &
Science Center

Old State
Capitol

SPANISH
TOWN

RIVER RD.

LAFAYETTE

N. 3RD

N. 5TH

N. 7TH

N. 9TH

CAPITOL ACCESS RD.

NORTH ST.

Old Governor's
Mansion

N. 4TH

CONVENTION ST.

110

Riverside
Centroplex

AMERICA ST.

LOUISIANA ST.

NORTH BLVD.

FLORIDA ST.

to
Plantation
Homes

GOVERNMENT ST.

10

TERRACE AVE.

3C

to Louisiana
State University

to Blue Bayou
Water Park

10

BATON ROUGE
Downtown

Animal lovers should be sure to visit the beautiful garden-like setting of the Greater Baton Rouge Zoo. This zoo contains more than 1,400 animals. It also has train rides, a children's zoo, and an aquarium featuring Louisiana fish and reptiles.

No visit to Baton Rouge would be complete without a trip through one of its mysterious bayous. Several organizations offer swamp tours in search of alligators. While cruising through the bayou, take note of the cypress trees and wildlife that make their homes in this rich and diverse habitat.

Alligators live in the southern lowlands of Louisiana. Adult male alligators can grow as long as 12 feet (4 m) and weigh up to 500 pounds (227 kg).

CHAPTER FIVE

THE PEOPLE AND PLACES OF LOUISIANA

More than four million people live in Louisiana. Just over half live in or near the big cities of New Orleans, Baton Rouge, and Shreveport. Many others live in mid-size cities such as Alexandria, Lafayette, Kenner, and Lake Charles. Some people prefer the quiet life of the many rural areas across the state.

Of all the states, Louisiana is perhaps the most diverse. The vast majority—about 60 in every 100 people—are descendants of the area's first European settlers. African-Americans make up the next largest ethnic group and number about 30 in every 100 people. Hispanics (2 in 100) and Asians (1 in 100), along with Cajuns, Creoles, Native Americans, and other races, make up the remainder of the population.

All of the ethnic groups who settled Louisiana made contributions to its rich culture and heritage. The African-American influence stands out. The distinct balconies of the French Quarter were hammered out by

A street artist sells her wares in New Orleans' Jackson Square.

SPECIAL LANGUAGE

Have you ever made up your own special words for you and your friends? Creole children did just that. They heard so many different languages that they weren't sure which one to use. So they made their own combinations of words. It turned into a language all its own—a combination of French, English, and West Indian. Now you can speak Creole, too!

English	French	Creole
Hello	Bonjour	Bonjou
Please	S'il vous plait	Si-to-ple
Thank you	Merci	Mersi
I'm sorry	Je regrette	Mo chagren
My name is	Je m'appelle	Mo pele
Good-bye	Au Revoir	Adyeu

African ironworkers. African-American music, such as jazz and reggae, is everywhere in Louisiana. Gospel music, which originated with African-Americans, is also popular there. Louisiana's Mahalia Jackson is a legendary gospel singer.

Two other groups have also had a unique influence on Louisiana: Creoles and Cajuns. Historically, the descendants of French, Spanish, or Portuguese people were called Creoles. Today, the meaning of the word "Creole" varies, but it often refers to the French-speaking population of European descent. Creole music is lively and uses a variety of instruments, including triangles, fiddles, spoons, and other things. Zydeco music was also born of the Creole community. The words of Zydeco music are sung in Creole French, accompanied by an accordion and a rub board.

Cajuns are just as lively. The Cajun motto is to eat, dance, and laugh; then, eat, dance, and laugh some more. Cajuns are descendants of the Acadians, who were French-Canadians living in Nova Scotia, Canada, in the 1600s. Many Acadians moved to Louisiana in the mid-1700s, and the word *Acadian* eventually became *Cajun*. There are about one-half

million Cajuns in Louisiana today. The combined cultures of the Cajuns and the Creoles continue to have a great influence on Louisiana today.

Of all the things Louisiana is known for, Mardi Gras may be the most popular. Mardi Gras is an ancient European celebration held in late February or early March. Often called the "Largest Free Show on Earth," it is an extravaganza of parades and parties. Partygoers wear masks and dress in fancy costume, and parade through the streets to show off their finery. Although Mardi Gras is actually just one day —46 days before Easter—the term is also used to refer to the carnival season, which begins on January 6th and ends on Mardi Gras.

Many traditions have developed surrounding Mardi Gras. The African Zulu Mardi Gras parade is world-famous. There are also neighborhood "tribes" of Mardi Gras Indians. They dress in colorful costumes

Louisiana artists, painters, and sculptors create colorful floats for Mardi Gras.

and fight mock battles on Mardi Gras Day. Although the most well-known celebration takes place in New Orleans, other communities throughout the state also celebrate Mardi Gras.

Louisiana provides products for the United States and beyond. It is the second largest producer of natural gas in the nation and the third top producer of oil. Workers are needed in manufacturing plants, service industries, and on oil rigs, among other places.

Manufacturing industries employ many people throughout the state. Chemicals are the leading manufactured product in Louisiana. Chemical products include plastics, fertilizers, paint, soap, and pharmaceuticals (medical drugs). The chief chemical production plants are located in Baton Rouge, Lake Charles, Shreveport, and New Orleans. The manufacturing of chemicals and other products such as paper are vital to Louisiana's economy.

Mining is also an important business in Louisiana. Petroleum refineries (places where oil is cleaned for future use) are located mainly in the southern part of the state. Large natural gas refineries are upstate near Monroe and Shreveport. Other mined products include sulfur, coal, sand, and gravel.

Louisiana is a farming state. Soybeans are its main crop. Healthful soy is used for nondairy milk and products such as tofu. Louisiana is the second largest producer of sweet potatoes in the nation, and it is also a leading producer of cotton. Louisiana farmers also grow rice, corn, fruit, vegetables, pecans, and—everyone's favorite—sugarcane, a chief source of sugar. Salt is another major product from Louisiana. The state has several natural islands made up of salt, including Avery Island, located in south central Louisiana near the Gulf of Mexico. The largest and oldest salt mine in the Western Hemisphere is on Avery Island.

The food industry is a major source of jobs in Louisiana. Some of the state's leading processed foods include coffee, sodas, and sugar. Konriko is America's oldest running rice mill. Another thriving business is Chef Paul Prudhomme's Magic Seasoning Blends, Inc., which sells spices used in authentic Louisiana cooking. Crystal® Hot Sauce, manufactured in Louisiana, is enjoyed the world over. Another famous Louisiana product is Tabasco® Pepper Sauce, produced by the McIlhenny family since 1868. This famous pepper sauce is a natural product using wild, hot peppers and salt from Avery Island. Visitors can take a tour of the Tabasco plant.

A woman picks peppers on Avery Island to be used for Tabasco® sauce.

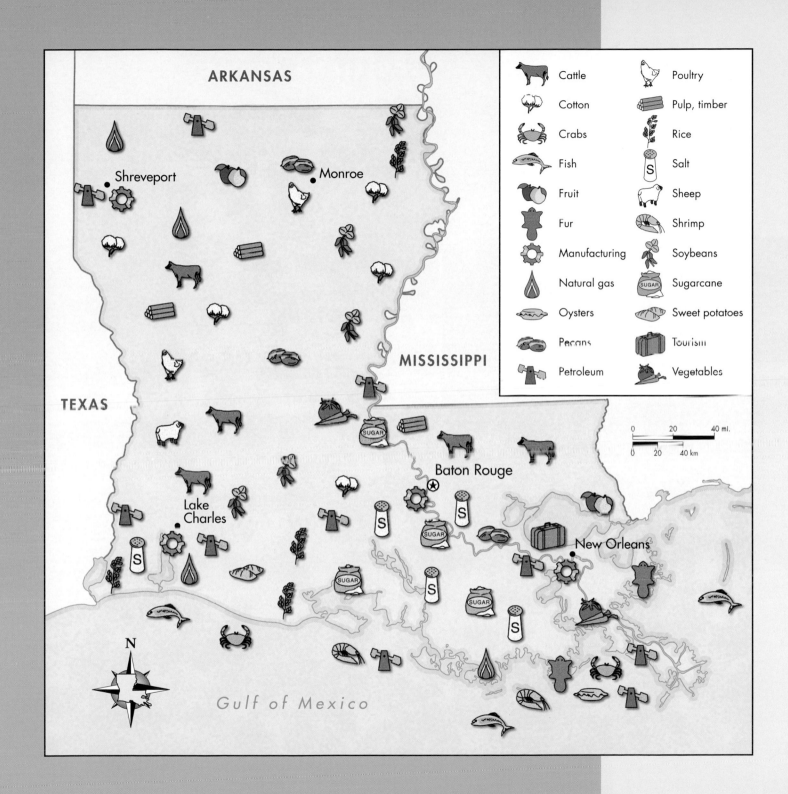

ARKANSAS

Shreveport

Monroe

MISSISSIPPI

TEXAS

Lake
Charles

Baton Rouge

New Orleans

Gulf of Mexico

N

	Cattle		Poultry
	Cotton		Pulp, timber
	Crabs		Rice
	Fish		Salt
	Fruit		Sheep
	Fur		Shrimp
	Manufacturing		Soybeans
	Natural gas		Sugarcane
	Oysters		Sweet potatoes
	Pecans		Tourism
	Petroleum		Vegetables

0   20   40 ml.
0   20   40 km

Some of Louisiana's most popular dishes are variations of jambalaya, a Cajun/Creole dish. To make jambalaya, rice is mixed with a variety of ingredients, such as beef, pork, chicken, sausage, or shrimp. No matter how you make it, one thing remains the same—jambalaya is delicious! Ask an adult for help to make the sausage jambalaya recipe below.

SAUSAGE JAMBALAYA

1 1/2 cups uncooked rice
1 to 2 lbs. smoked sausage, sliced
1 medium onion, chopped
3 to 5 stalks celery, chopped
1 medium bell pepper, diced
2 cloves garlic, chopped (optional)
salt and pepper to taste
vegetable oil

1. Brown sausage and vegetables in oil.
2. Add seasonings and saute about 5 minutes.
3. Add rice and stir in 3 cups water. Bring to a boil.
4. Cover and lower heat. Simmer 30 to 45 minutes or until rice is done.

Products from Louisiana and around the world must be transported to other places, creating many more jobs within the state. Ships come in through ports along the Gulf of Mexico or the Mississippi River, bringing goods in and taking goods out. Shipbuilders are in constant demand to build new vessels. Mechanics and deckhands keep ships in good running order. River pilots maneuver boats along passageways. Other jobs in the transportation industry include businesses designed around aircraft, automobile, and truck manufacturing and maintenance.

Louisiana's aquaculture industry is also booming. Aquaculture is the growing and harvesting of fish in a contained environment such as a tank. Louisiana aquaculture includes oysters, shrimp, crabs, and crawfish. Louisiana is the largest producer of tasty oysters and crawfish in the nation. About 100 million pounds (45 million kilograms) of crawfish or "little lobsters" are produced per year, half of which comes from the Atchafalaya Basin. Louisianans eat their little lobsters by the handful. The Swedish are also big fans—Sweden buys 2,500 tons (2,540 metric tons) of Louisiana crawfish every year.

EXTRA! EXTRA!

Aquaculture in Louisiana now includes alligators. Alligator farmers raise these once endangered reptiles for their meat and skins, which are used to make shoes and purses. Animal rights activists are trying to stop alligator killings.

Southern Louisiana is the crawfish capital of the world.

Let's begin our tour in Louisiana's most famous city, New Orleans. New Orleans alone receives five million tourists every year—more than the number of residents in the entire state! Once called Crescent City, New Orleans is also referred to as the Cradle of Jazz, the Queen City of the South, and the Big Easy.

New Orleans has as many attractions as it does names. First, hop on the St. Charles Streetcar to the French Quarter, the only "European town" in the United States. The French Quarter contains 90 blocks and 2,700 buildings. With its many outside cafes and elegant brick buildings, the French Quarter was designed to look and feel like a true French city.

The French Quarter is considered by many to be the heart of New Orleans.

While the setting may be French, the music is American. Venture down Bourbon Street to hear traditional Dixieland music. There's always a show at the historic Preservation Hall, the showcase for the Preservation Hall Jazz band.

Watch the ships come in as you stroll along Riverwalk Marketplace, a series of restaurants and shops overlooking the Mississippi River. Then take a drive over the Lake Pontchartrain Causeway. It is 24 miles (39 km) long, making it the longest over-water bridge in the world. If you're in the mood for inspiration, visit St. Louis Cathedral in bustling Jackson Square, or the elegant Degas House, where artist Edgar Degas created at least seventeen incredible paintings. Degas was known for his portraits of ballet dancers.

In New Orleans, the struggle for civil rights is not forgotten at places such as the U.S. Customs House, a headquarters built by African-Americans before the Civil War; and the Cabildo, the colonial capitol that now houses African-American artifacts, or objects from long ago.

While in New Orleans, dare to explore the "Cities of the Dead," the famous

above-ground cemeteries. Above-ground burials were always a custom in Spain. The custom was brought to Louisiana in the 1800s, when the territory was under Spanish rule. Many of the raised tombs have statues and fancy decorations. Visitors can take a guided tour of an above-ground cemetery at night, when the setting is most spooky!

Next, check out the Jean Lafitte & Bayou Sauvage National Wildlife Refuge. You may be surprised to find wild hogs, raccoons, rabbits, minks, muskrats, deer, snakes, frogs, giant turtles, birds (including pelicans), and otters in the big city of New Orleans.

Many above-ground tombs hold the remains of several generations of family members.

West Gulf Coastal Plain

The West Gulf Coastal Plain, which makes up the largest portion of the state, has many interesting sights. Learn how the Creoles and Cajuns lived by cruising along the Cane River to see old Creole architecture. The 33-block National Historic Landmark District in Natchitoches displays a vast collection of Creole mud dwellings from the early days of European settlement. The 180-mile (290-km) Creole Nature Trail meanders through central Louisiana. It is Louisiana's only National Scenic Byway and an official All-American Road.

A collection of Cajun homes is available for viewing at Acadian Village in Lafayette. Lafayette is part of St. Landry parish, home of the

WHO'S WHO IN LOUISIANA?

Anne Rice (1941–) is the best-selling author of *Interview With the Vampire* and many other novels. Her books often have eerie Louisiana settings and mysterious characters such as vampires. Rice was born in New Orleans and lives in the Garden District.

Acadian Village includes Acadian homes from the 1800s, as well as a blacksmith shop, a general store, and a chapel.

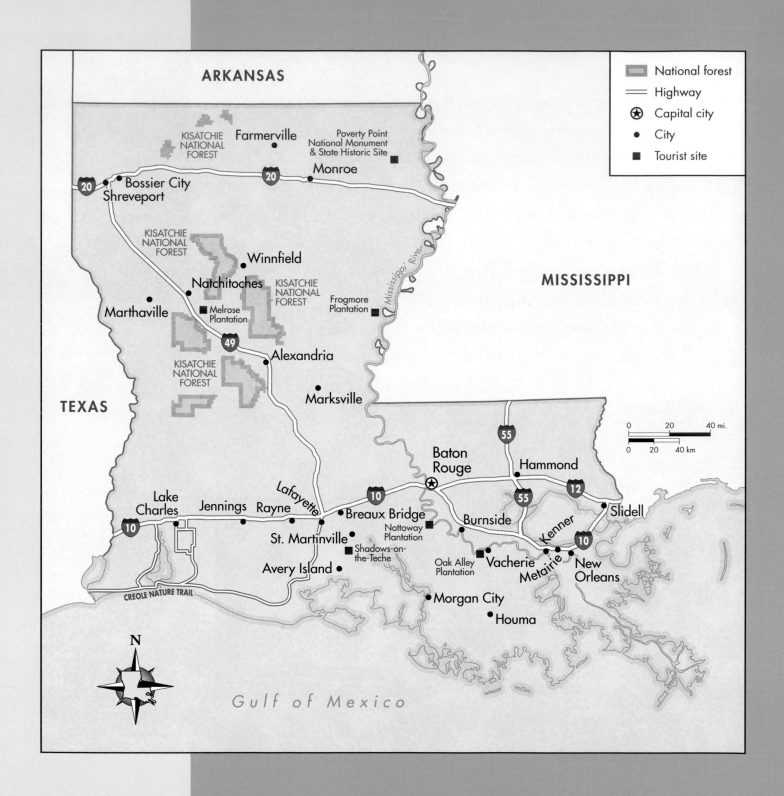

ARKANSAS

KISATCHIE NATIONAL FOREST

Farmerville

Poverty Point National Monument & State Historic Site

Monroe

Bossier City

Shreveport

KISATCHIE NATIONAL FOREST

Winnfield

Natchitoches

KISATCHIE NATIONAL FOREST

Marthaville

Melrose Plantation

Frogmore Plantation

MISSISSIPPI

Mississippi River

Alexandria

KISATCHIE NATIONAL FOREST

Marksville

TEXAS

Baton Rouge

Hammond

Lafayette

Lake Charles

Jennings

Rayne

Breaux Bridge

Burnside

Slidell

St. Martinville

Nottoway Plantation

Kenner

Shadows-on-the-Teche

Oak Alley Plantation

Vacherie

New Orleans

Avery Island

Metairie

CREOLE NATURE TRAIL

Morgan City

Houma

N

Gulf of Mexico

National forest

Highway

Capital city

City

Tourist site

zydeco. Zydeco is a type of music that is played with assorted objects such as knobs, forks, or anything that makes an interesting sound. It was invented in St. Landry. For more of the Cajun experience, eat crawfish (also called mudbugs) in the "Crawfish Capital of the World," Breaux Bridge.

Avery Island should be known as the egret capital of the world. If it wasn't for Tabasco® founder Edmund McIlhenny's son, Edward, Louisiana might not have egrets. Egrets had been hunted almost to extinction for their snowy white feathers. In 1892, Edward "Mr. Ned" McIlhenny saved seven egrets, starting a colony at his home on Avery Island. He called it Bird City. Seven grew to 100,000, the largest population of egrets in the nation. Mr. Ned later created Jungle Gardens for rare plants and flowers.

After all that activity, take a rest under the Evangeline Oak in St. Martinville. This now famous tree inspired Henry Wadsworth Longfellow's poem about Gabriel and Evangeline. The characters are often called the Cajun Romeo and Juliet, after the star-crossed lovers of William Shakespeare's classic play.

For Native American history, the Tunica-Biloxi Museum and Reservation at Marksville has mounds and artifacts from

Each spring, snowy egrets nest on pier-like structures in Bird City.

civilizations more than two thousand years old. The Louisiana State Exhibit Museum in Shreveport has a fine collection of artifacts from the peaceful Caddo group. The Mississippi Mud Museum has warrior spears used before the birth of Christ.

Historic African-American sites are scattered throughout Louisiana. The very first one was the Arna Bontemps African-American Museum and Cultural Center in Alexandria, named for a writer who lived in the 1930s. The Stephens African-American Museum is in Shreveport, and the Northeast Louisiana Delta African-American Museum is in Monroe.

Plantations make history come alive. They show how slaves lived and worked. Interesting plantations include the Melrose Plantation (formerly the Yucca Plantation) and the Frogmore Plantation, a working cotton plantation with slave cabins dating back to 1810.

No visit to Louisiana is complete without a few ghost stories. Ghosts seem to be regular visitors on plantations. Loyd Hall near Alexandria is reportedly haunted by a redheaded, violin-playing, Confederate spy. At Chretien Point Plantation, a widowed woman shot a pirate dead as he climbed her staircase. Some visitors have reported seeing a mysterious dark figure that may be the pirate wandering around at night. More ghosts can be found in Hanging Square in Farmerville, where wrongdoers were hanged in public.

Civil War buffs may want to visit Marthaville to pay their respects to the Grave of the Unknown Confederate Soldier. This soldier was killed

(opposite)
You can learn about Louisiana history by touring the state's many plantations.

by Union troops in April 1864. Still more history can be found at the Louisiana Political Museum in Winnfield. The museum is filled with items relating to Louisiana politicians, including Louisiana's favorite son, Governor Huey P. "the Kingfish" Long.

Are you ready for signs of life? Drive north to Sportsman's Paradise over the Caddo Lake Drawbridge, the last surviving "vertical-lift" bridge in Louisiana. The bridge was designed so that the center would lift up, allowing tall oil equipment to pass through. Animal lovers will enjoy the Chateau des Cocodries (French/Cajun for "House of Alligators") in Jennings. Natchitoches offers the Bayou Pierre Gator Park and Show.

Mississippi Alluvial Plain

Native Americans once lived along the rich banks of the Mississippi River. As a result, the Mississippi Alluvial Plain is home to several fascinating Native American sites. At Poverty Point, you can see pottery, cooking balls, and arrowheads used by prehistoric Mound Builders who lived long before ancient Roman and Greek civilizations.

Plantations also thrived along the Mississippi River. The River Road African-American Museum near Burnside shows the African-American experience both before and after slavery. The Houmas House, also in Burnside, was purchased by European settlers from the Houmas Indians. It was established as a sugarcane plantation in 1800. Many visitors come to see this restored establishment with its beautiful mansion.

The Oak Alley Plantation is probably the most popular plantation in all of Louisiana, partly because of its spectacular setting. Visitors to Oak Alley have fun trying to find the answers to these mysterious ques-

An impressive row of giant oak trees forms an "oak alley" at this famous plantation.

tions: Why are the clocks stopped? Why is there a pineapple at the foot of the bed?

The Laura Plantation in Vacherie is another popular historic site. This Creole plantation was built in 1805 and is noted for its fine craftsmanship. The famous Br'er Rabbit story, an old African legend, was believed to have been introduced by the slaves who worked at Laura Plantation. The old Disney movie, "Song of the South," tells the story of Br'er Rabbit and his friends.

East Gulf Coastal Plain

There are more ghosts to be found on this side of Louisiana. Shadows-on-the-Teche supposedly contains its own plantation ghost. Its identity may be uncovered by reading the 17,000 letters, photos, and recipes on display there. Another mysterious spot is the Myrtles. Find out why the mirrors are covered and why it is called "the most haunted house in America."

It may be time for some fresh air. The drive along Bayou Lafourche provides many scenic sights of wetlands and wildlife. As always, watch for alligator crossing signs. Oakley House is a great place for bird watching. How many birds can you watch at Oakley House? John James Audubon painted eighty bird portraits there.

There's always something to do and see in Louisiana. Some people come in search of excitement, having heard tales of voodoo, vampires, and ghosts. What they find is beautiful scenery, great music, and friendly people. The simple truth is that anyone who has experienced Louisiana never really leaves. The memories last forever.

LOUISIANA ALMANAC

Statehood date and number: April 30, 1812/18th

State seal: Inner circle has a golden pelican feeding three chicks in a nest. They are encircled by the words: "Union, Justice, Confidence." Outer circle is blue with the words "State of Louisiana." Adopted April 30, 1902.

State flag: Blue flag with white pelican atop a banner with the state motto. Adopted in 1912.

Geographic center: Avoyelles, 3 miles (4.8 km) southeast of Marksville

Total area/rank: 49,650 square miles (128,593 sq km)/31st

Coastline: 397 miles (639 km)

Borders: Texas, Arkansas, Mississippi, Gulf of Mexico

Longitude and latitude: Louisiana is located at approximately 31.09° N and 92.05° W.

Highest/lowest elevation: 535 feet (163 m), Driskill Mountain/8 feet (2.4 m) below sea level, New Orleans

Hottest/coldest temperature: 114° F (46° C) on August 10, 1936 at Plain Dealing/–16° F (–27° C) on February 13, 1899 at Minden

Land area/rank: 43,566 square miles (112,800 sq km)/33rd

Inland water area/rank: 4,153 square miles (10,756 sq km)/5th

Population/rank: 4,468,976/22nd

Population of major cities:
   New Orleans: 484,674
   Baton Rouge: 227,818
   Shreveport: 200,145

Origin of state name: Named by René-Robert Cavelier, Sieur de La Salle, for King Louis XIV of France

State capital: Baton Rouge

Previous capitals: New Orleans, Donaldsonville, Opelousas, Shreveport

Parishes: 64

State government: 39 senators, 105 representatives

Major rivers/lakes: Mississippi River, Red River, Atchafalaya River, Sabine River, Pearl River/Lake Pontchartrain, Toledo Bend Lake

Farm products: Sugar, strawberries, sweet potatoes, rice, corn, pecans

Livestock: Beef and dairy cattle, sheep, goats, pigs

Manufactured products: Paper, wood, chemicals, oil products, food, plastics, metals

Mining products: Petroleum, natural gas, carbon, gravel, sulfur, salt

Fishing products: Shrimp, crawfish, oysters, crabs, bass, white perch, red tail snapper

Amphibian: Green tree frog

Bird: Eastern brown pelican

Crustacean: Crawfish

Dog: Catahoula leopard dog

Drink: Milk

Flower: Magnolia

Gemstone: Agate

Insect: Honey bee

Mammal: Black bear

Motto: Union, Justice, and Confidence

Nicknames: Pelican State, Bayou State, Creole State, Sugar State, Cradle of Jazz, Sportsman's Paradise

Reptile: Alligator

Songs: "Give Me Louisiana" (words and music by Doralice Fontane); "You Are My Sunshine" (words and music by Jimmie Davis and Charles Mitchell)

Tree: Bald cypress

Wildflower: Louisiana iris

Wildlife: Egrets, bald eagles, alligators, pelicans, beavers, turtles

TIME**LINE**

LOUISIANA STATE **HISTORY**

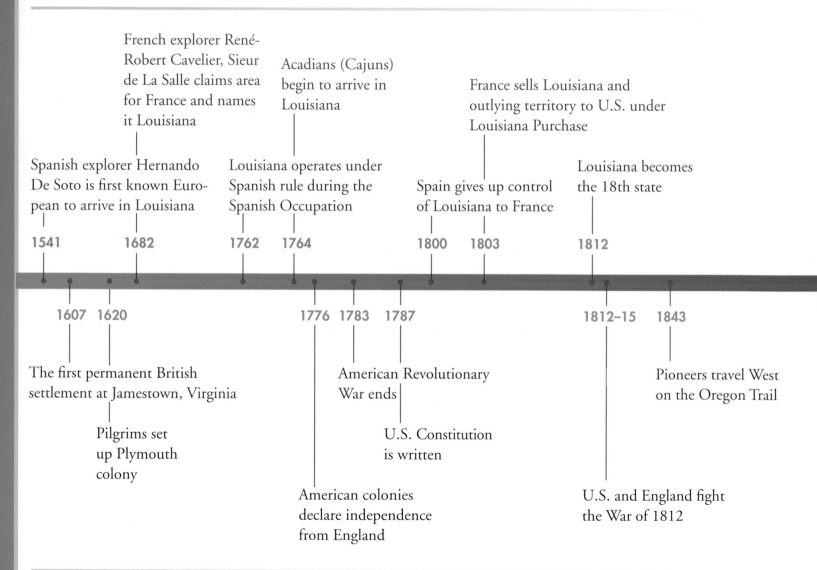

French explorer René-
Robert Cavelier, Sieur
de La Salle claims area
for France and names
it Louisiana

Acadians (Cajuns)
begin to arrive in
Louisiana

France sells Louisiana and
outlying territory to U.S. under
Louisiana Purchase

Spanish explorer Hernando
De Soto is first known European to arrive in Louisiana

Louisiana operates under
Spanish rule during the
Spanish Occupation

Spain gives up control
of Louisiana to France

Louisiana becomes
the 18th state

1541   **1682**   **1762**   **1764**   **1800**   **1803**   **1812**

1607 1620   **1776 1783 1787**   **1812–15 1843**

The first permanent British
settlement at Jamestown, Virginia

American Revolutionary
War ends

Pioneers travel West
on the Oregon Trail

Pilgrims set
up Plymouth
colony

U.S. Constitution
is written

American colonies
declare independence
from England

U.S. and England fight
the War of 1812

UNITED STATES **HISTORY**

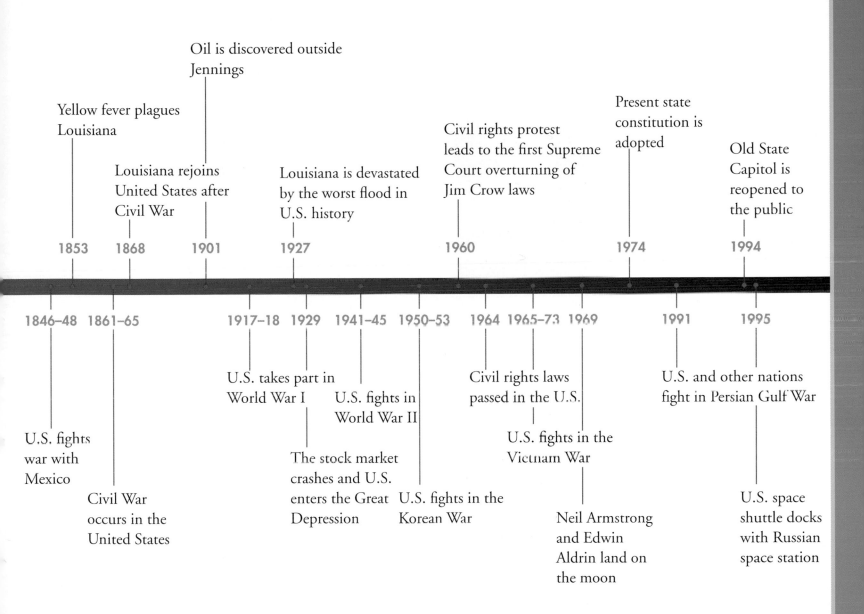

Oil is discovered outside Jennings

Yellow fever plagues Louisiana

Louisiana rejoins United States after Civil War

Louisiana is devastated by the worst flood in U.S. history

Civil rights protest leads to the first Supreme Court overturning of Jim Crow laws

Present state constitution is adopted

Old State Capitol is reopened to the public

1853   1868   1901   1927   1960   1974   1994

1846–48   1861–65   1917–18 1929 1941–45 1950–53   1964 1965–73 1969   1991   1995

U.S. takes part in World War I

U.S. fights in World War II

Civil rights laws passed in the U.S.

U.S. and other nations fight in Persian Gulf War

U.S. fights war with Mexico

The stock market crashes and U.S. enters the Great Depression

U.S. fights in the Korean War

U.S. fights in the Vietnam War

Civil War occurs in the United States

Neil Armstrong and Edwin Aldrin land on the moon

U.S. space shuttle docks with Russian space station

73

GALLERY OF FAMOUS LOUISIANANS

Terry Bradshaw

(1948–)

Popular television sportscaster and former quarterback for the Pittsburgh Steelers. He was twice named Super Bowl Most Valuable Player and is a member of the Pro Football Hall of Fame. Born in Shreveport.

Harry Connick Jr.

(1967–)

Accomplished composer and performer; Grammy award winner. Born in New Orleans.

Fats Domino

(1928–)

Blues singer and pioneer rock and roll singer. Songs include "Blueberry Hill" and "Ain't That a Shame." Born in New Orleans.

Ernest Gaines

(1933–)

Award-winning author of *A Lesson Before Dying,* and *The Autobiography of Miss Jane Pittman.* Writer-in-resident at University of Southwestern Louisiana. Born in Oscar.

Shirley Ann Grau

(1929–)

Novel and short-story author, Pulitzer Prize fiction winner. Her books contain Louisiana settings and themes such as Creole descendants. Born in New Orleans.

Wynton Marsalis

(1961–)

Modern jazz artist, trumpet player, and bandleader. His father, Ellis, is a jazz pianist, and his brother, Branford, is a jazz saxophonist. Born in New Orleans.

Aaron Neville

(1941–)

Blues singer, zydeco musician, and Neville Brothers band member. Born in New Orleans.

Corinne Boggs "Cokie" Roberts

(1943–)

Award-winning television journalist, author, and National Public Radio correspondent. Her parents were Louisiana congress-persons. Born in New Orleans.

Britney Spears

(1981–)

Pop singer and platinum-selling recording artist. Born and raised in Kentwood.

GLOSSARY

activist: someone willing to work for a special cause, to bring about change

amendment: change or addition to an existing law

artifact: simple object or tool from an older, often ancient, civilization

assassinated: murdered suddenly or secretively, usually for political reasons

balmy: mild and warm; refers to weather

colony: a land or place settled by a group of people from another country, who are ruled by their home country; also refers to a group of animals (e.g., egrets) living in isolation from other species

descendant: a person (e.g., grandchild) who follows a previous group

economy: a system of producing and distributing goods

extravaganza: a big, overdone party or celebration

humid: moisture and wetness in the air

jambalaya: spicy mixture of rice and various seafood

marshland: land that is soft and wet

masonry: built of stone or brick

melting pot: phrase used to indicate a blending of many cultures

mock: fake or pretend

motto: a phrase or saying that sums up a group's or individual's purpose

obstacle: something that stands in the way

tourist: a visitor from another place

plantation: a large farm that usually grows one main crop

renovation: the process of restoring or repairing something

siege: an attempt to isolate and attack a protected area

veto: to cancel a previously approved law or proposal

voodoo: a religion (originally from Africa) that uses spells and charms and is practiced mainly in Haiti

FOR MORE INFORMATION

Web sites

Discover Louisiana
www.louisianatravel.com
Information about Louisiana attractions and accomodations.

Audubon Louisiana Nature Center
http://www.auduboninstitute.org/Inc/index.htm
Information about and photographs of the nature institute.

Info Louisiana
www.state.la.us/index.htm
The official state web site.

Books

Gravelle, Karen and Sylviane Diouf. *Growing Up In Crawfish Country: A Cajun Childhood.* Danbury, CT: Franklin Watts, 1998.

Hiscock, Bruce. *The Big Rivers: The Missouri, the Mississippi, and the Ohio.* New York, NY: Atheneum, 1997.

Macmillan, Dianne. *Mardi Gras.* Springfield, NJ: Enslow, 1997.

Medearis, Angela Shelf. *Little Louis and the Jazz Band: The Story of Louis "Satchmo" Armstrong.* New York, NY: Lodestar Books, 1994.

Addresses

Office of the Governor
Attn: Constituent Services
P. O. Box 94004
Baton Rouge, LA 70804-9004

Office of State Library
P. O. Box 131
Baton Rouge, LA 70821-0131

Office of State Parks
P. O. Box 44426
Baton Rouge, LA 70804-4426

Office of Tourism
P. O. Box 94291
Baton Rouge, LA 70804-9291

INDEX

ABOUT THE AUTHOR

Ellen Macaulay has always found Louisiana to be a fascinating, colorful state. She researched this book by reading lots of other books and checking out web sites. Ellen would like to thank her speedy research assistants, Robert and Colin Macaulay, Carol, and everyone at the San Mateo Library Reference Desk, Tabasco's Dr. Shane Bernard, and Louisiana State librarian, Judy Smith. Throughout the process, Ellen discovered that the best research was in talking to or reading about people who have experienced Louisiana. Many people love Louisiana and are happy to share their stories.